GOD

PLAYS GOLF!

GOD
PLAYS GOLF!

DAVID CURRY

W

WHITAKER
HOUSE

GOD PLAYS GOLF!

David Curry
The Foundation for Grace
P.O. Box 6943
Tacoma, WA 98406
www.Godplaysgolf.com
david.curry@earthlink.com

ISBN: 0-88368-879-4
Printed in the United States of America
© 2001, 2003 by David Curry

Whitaker House
30 Hunt Valley Circle
New Kensington, PA 15068
visit our web site: www.whitakerhouse.com

Library of Congress Cataloging-in-Publication Data

Curry, David, 1968–
  God plays golf! / David Curry.
     p.   cm.
  ISBN 0-88368-879-4 (pbk. : alk. paper)
  1. Golfers—Religious life.   2. Golf—Religious aspects—
Christianity.   3. Christian life. I. Title.
  BV4596.G64 C87 2003
  248.8'8—dc21
                                            2002154455

1 2 3 4 5 6 7 8 9 10 11 12 / 10 09 08 07 06 05 04 03

Acknowledgments

I would like to thank the members of my "book team," Leo Morin, Mary Johnson, and Sandy Endof-Horn. They are great friends and a great help. Thank you so much.

A special thank you to my sister, Becky Dela Cruz. Not only is she the Foundation for Grace office manager, she is my partner in all I do and deserves as much credit for this book as I do. (Although I won't put her name on the cover!)

My love and appreciation go to my wife, Kathleen, and our boys, Jack and Cole. They are my true loves.

Dedication

*This book is dedicated to the other members
of my favorite golf foursome:
Dean, John, and Sharon.*

*They are always making me look
like a better golfer than I am.
I dream of the day
we will all play the fairway
on the same hole.*

Contents

Before You Tee Off...An Introduction....... 11

Chapter 1: Improving Your Grip.............. 19

Chapter 2: Playing the Fairway................29

Chapter 3: Sand Traps
            and Water Hazards 41

Chapter 4: Mulligans, Handicaps,
            and Gimmes 49

Chapter 5: Making Solid Contact............ 61

Chapter 6: Playing in a Foursome 73

Chapter 7: The Clubhouse...................... 81

How to Use This Book 89

About the Author 93

Before You Tee Off...An Introduction

Before You Tee Off...
An Introduction

Does God really play golf? You will have to read this book to find out. Perhaps it is just a hunch; I certainly can't prove it theologically, but I do believe that God enjoys golf. I say this because golf is a tremendous metaphor for life. There are biblical principles that are more easily understood in light of a golf analogy. This book is about helping people navigate their questions about God and discover life-changing principles through the lens of golf. It is about helping you see the amazing parallels between a great round of golf and a great life. I know that both are possible, although at times both can be elusive.

For some people, golf is not an analogy for religion; it *is* a religion. There are many sports that have developed a loyal following. People pay big bucks to get courtside seats at a basketball game or a luxury box that gives them a great view from the fifty-yard line at a football game. But there is no comparison to the lifelong passion that golfers feel for their sport. The reasons for this are many. One of the greatest golfers of all time, Arnold Palmer, summed up the allure of golf better than I ever could.

> "Golf is deceptively simple and endlessly complicated. It satisfies the soul and frustrates the intellect. It is at the same time rewarding and maddening—It is without a doubt the greatest game that mankind has ever created."
> —Arnold Palmer

Because of the simplicity and complex nature of golf, those who get caught in its grasp are forever trying to figure out what skills, attitudes, and strategies they will need to conquer it. Few people ever master the game of golf, yet we all keep coming back for more punishment—sure that one day we will attain the level of proficiency that we strive toward. The entire idea is to take the ball from point A (the tee box) to point B (the green) in the most direct path, with the fewest possible strokes. Simple—right? Then why is golf so difficult and frustrating? Why do so many of us struggle to master this simple game? The answer is that golf is, in truth, often *complex* and rarely linear. The best possible shot is not always to hit the ball directly at the pin but, for example, to lay up just right of the green and use a different approach shot.

The difficulty level of golf requires that we use strategy and techniques to improve our game and to help us better understand how to play the course. Golfers call the skill of knowing how to approach each hole, "course management." There have been many golfers who have approached golf with the simple philosophy of "grip it and rip it"—hit the ball as long and as far as you can. Some have done it with a degree of success, but most have just gotten themselves into trouble and hazards. The greatest players have taken a more measured approach and asked themselves some key questions. One of these key questions is, "How did the course designer intend for this hole to be played to achieve par?"

The fact of the matter is that most people could use some "course management" for their lives. The truth is that there is a Designer of this place called Earth, and He has a design for each of us. Many of us would benefit by asking ourselves the question:

"How was this life designed to be lived for maximum happiness?"

While golf is a multi-faceted sport, simple and difficult at the same time, so too is life. As some great golfers have struggled because they have adopted a "grip it and rip it" mentality toward their game, some people have failed by adopting the same attitude toward life. They live as though life were all about things physical and monetary. But the *best* parts of life are the things you cannot see. They are spiritual and emotional.

Many people struggle with the spiritual part of life. This book is designed to help golfers understand the parallels between succeeding on the golf course and succeeding in the spiritual part of life. Over the centuries, people have made so many crazy claims about Jesus that one can easily be confused about who He was and what He said.

The life of Jesus Christ has been made to be far more complicated than it actually was. What He stood for and what He said in the Bible can be easily understood by the common man. You do not need to be a theologian or a "Jesus freak" to know, understand, and accept the words of Christ. It is quite simple. Yet, like golf, there is also a level of depth to what He said that can make His words applicable and infinitely practical for you and me today, even though they were written centuries ago.

This book contains some of the words of Jesus. If you read these words carefully, you will begin to get a picture of what and who Jesus was. It is important that you discover for yourself who Jesus was and not assume that you already know what He said and stood for. Just as many people think they have golf figured out (because they know that they are supposed to put the ball in the cup), so many people believe they already understand Christianity. There is more to Jesus than the flawed version you may have gotten from today's society. I encourage you to keep an open mind as you read what this little book has to say about playing the "game of life" for maximum fulfillment.

And who am I? A professional golfer perhaps? Sadly, no. I am just a simple player like you. I fell in love with the game of golf at the age of sixteen. While I make no claims to be a master of the game, I have had success at the game of life. In fact, spiritually speaking, I am a bit of a coach. I have spent the last eleven years helping people understand the words of Christ and what they mean. Just like you, there are times when I don't play the game of golf, or the game of life, perfectly. But through my understanding of golf I have come to understand the importance of a good coach.

For years, I have struggled to figure out what was wrong with my swing. One day I would play great, and the next I would suffer through the torture of "one of those days." Yet from the time I picked up the game of golf until the age of thirty-two, I never took a lesson. What a huge mistake! I wasted so much time. Likewise, there are many people who have deep questions about life, yet they never take the time to get the perspective of a coach. Just remember that the better golfer you are, the more likely you are to rely heavily upon coaching. People like Tiger Woods have personal coaches who break down their swing piece by piece. In the same way, the more you aspire to personal fulfillment and spiritual wisdom, the more you need to think about the subjects of God and eternity. Consulting with a pastor, reading a book like this, and reading the Bible can help direct you in the path that is best for you. Life is too important to try to solve on your own. My hope is that you will let this book be an inspiration to you on your spiritual journey.

1

Improving Your Grip

Improving Your Grip

Years ago I was teeing off with a group of friends that I had met at church. We had played basketball together as a group but had never had a chance to hit the links. I admit that when we got out on the course that day I was a little worried. These guys were big and athletic, and I felt there was a very good chance that I was going to get left behind. While I can't remember how I scored that day, I still remember how one of our foursome played. For the sake of this story, let's call him Sean. (Golf is humiliating enough, why make it worse by printing his actual name?)

Sean was a tremendously strong individual. When he stepped up to the tee, I fully expected him to whack the ball right up the middle. But as he addressed the ball, he faced toward the green and then turned forty-five degrees to the left. He was heading for the trees that lined the fairway! The entire group instantly broke up in laughter. "What are you doing?" I asked. He went on to explain that he suffered from a horrible slice. The only way he could hit the ball into the fairway was to hit it directly toward the trees and let it slice right back into the fairway. And so he did. He hit the ball directly at the trees and it sliced right into the fairway. The only problem was, as all golfers know, you can never rely on a slice. In key points of the round, just when he was depending on his slice, he would "acciden-tally" hit the ball straight—250 yards in the wrong direction! It would have been much easier to just figure out the fundamental prob-lem with his swing. Was it his grip? Perhaps it was his stance? We may never know. Last I heard, he was still aiming for the woods.

One of the most important things needed to succeed as a golfer is getting the correct grip. It is a fundamental part of golf. Without the correct grip, you have lost valuable strokes before you have even swung the club! It is almost as though you are doomed to struggle if you can't figure out how to hold the club correctly. Over the years, I have seen countless varieties of golf grips. Some of them were comical. There are any number of ways a person can hold the club, especially when putting. The issue of grip comes down to one main principle: To succeed, you must have an understanding of the fundamentals of the game of golf. Without an understanding of the fundamentals of the game, everything that is built upon them will be forever flawed.

It is equally important to have a strong foundational understanding of God and of the reason you and I need to have a personal relationship with Jesus Christ. Without this basic understanding, the words and claims of Jesus will not have the same depth of meaning for you. Just as with the fundamentals of golf, everything in Christianity is built upon the understanding of three basic ideas.

Foundational Truths...

...God exists.
This is the first biblical truth concerning the nature of God. Some people find it

interesting to discover that the Bible never tries to prove that God exists. It simply affirms that God is real, that He really does exist. Surveys suggest that most Americans believe that God exists; they just don't always agree on who God is. Over the years, I have had a chance to talk with many people who would not consider themselves to be "religious" people, yet they had a deep belief in God. I always consider this to be a positive sign that people are thinking about the important issues of life. So much of what and who we are is rooted in the spiritual and emotional connections we have. Failing to deal with the spiritual part of your life would be similar to ignoring an overdue electric bill. Eventually you will have to pay that bill or suffer the consequences of having your electricity shut off. Many people have ignored their spiritual life to their own detriment.

Years ago, I was asked to officiate at a funeral for an elderly gentleman who had passed away. He was a first-class guy and a terrific golfer. By all accounts, he was a responsible citizen. He had taken care of his family financially and always showed up for work. But he was a person who had ignored the role of God in his life. He felt it was not important and that religious people were all a bunch of hypocrites. At the end of his funeral, one of his friends made a statement that I will not forget. At the close of the service, he said to me and some of the others who were in attendance, "Golf was his religion. When he was out on the course, that was as close as he came to experiencing God." While I understood his deep love of golf, I could not help but feel that he had missed so much by not addressing the issue of God in his life.

The beginning of every spiritual journey starts with the internal questions: Is there a God? Who is God? Can I know Him? Many people would answer, "Yes. There is a God," but never stop to consider what that means to them. If you consider yourself to be someone who has belief in God but have never thought of how that may affect your life, then you are in the right place, because this book will help you walk through this process. If you are one of many people who have no previous belief in God, then this is a good place for *you* to begin, too! The Bible always addresses the issue of unbelief with a simple formula. The formula is this: Take a look.

Examine the historical Jesus and the words He spoke. The Bible assures those with doubts that, if they search for God, He can easily be found.

...God is love.

This is the second biblical truth about God. His very nature is approachable and loving. From the very beginning, God showed His loving nature toward us. In the book of Genesis, we read that human beings were created to have a relationship with God. He wanted to know you and me. Throughout the Bible, it is clear that the only thing God really wants from you is your love and attention. The most famous Bible verse, John 3:16, says this:

> *For God so loved the world that he gave his only Son, so that everyone who believes in him will not perish but have eternal life.*

A renowned theologian once said that the first chapter of the Bible could accurately be summarized, "God so loved that He gave the world." God is love from the beginning to the end.

But anyone who does not love does not know God—for God is love.

(1 John 4:8)

If God is love, why do so many people struggle to recognize this fact? Well, certainly some people would agree with the elderly golfer I mentioned in the previous story who thought Christians were hypocrites. History has taught us that religious people are not always loving and Christlike. Some people have drawn conclusions about God's nature from observing the nature of Christians. However, it is difficult and inaccurate to judge anything by its abuses and misled followers.

Some years ago, I was having a conversation with my wife about a recent round of golf. With a great deal of exasperation and enthusiasm, I discussed my performance. When I finished telling her about all the difficulties I'd had that day, she asked me a question, "Why do you even bother going out there?" I looked at her with shock and amazement. "Because I love that stupid game." She had misread my actions to conclude that golf was a big waste of time. (She has since changed her mind.) The analogy is obvious. A bad experience with a

Christian should not influence your concept of God. The nature of God is loving and approachable. He wants to communicate and have a relationship with you and me.

...God always does the right thing.

This is the third biblical truth about God. In theological terms, the word to describe Him is *righteous*. This is important because it reveals a problem most of us face in our relationship with God. We believe in Him, yet we know that we cannot measure up to His standard of goodness. Even at our best, we are still humans with imperfections and shortcomings.

Over the years, I have had occasion to play golf with people who had a great deal of fear about certain holes. I myself have played certain holes that were so difficult that I felt as though I were cursed. The chances of me making par seemed slim. When faced with that kind of situation, many people get discouraged. For a short period of time, it takes the fun out of the game—if you let it.

That is the way some people feel about the goodness of God. They realize that they are not worthy of that kind of perfection, and it just serves to frustrate them. But God doesn't intend for His goodness to frustrate you; instead, He wants it to give you confidence in Him. What good is it to try to have a relationship with a God who cannot be trusted to do the right thing? Because God always does the right thing, we are able to count on Him to be just and fair with us. We know that He holds us all to the same standards. He doesn't play favorites. He has a plan to help us with our inability to meet His standards.

> *For all have sinned; all fall short of God's glorious standard. Yet now God in his gracious kindness declares us not guilty. He has done this through Christ Jesus, who has freed us by taking away our sins.*
> (Romans 3:23–24)

2

Playing the Fairway

Playing the Fairway

Golf is infinitely more fun when you are playing the fairway. I have spent a good deal of my golf life somewhere deep in the woods. When I go golfing, I am usually required to bring a three-day ration of food, just in case I get lost. Well, it might not be that bad, but there is a big difference in my level of fulfillment when I am in the fairway as opposed to the rough. Years ago, I thought about printing up some T-shirts that said, "Only Wimps Play the Fairway." I probably could have made a million dollars had I done it. If you beat me to it, more power to you. Just give me credit.

In real life, many people like to think of themselves as creative and daring because they live life on the edge. Everything in life is a challenge for these people. They want to do it their way, whether it works or not. That is not creativity—that is chaos. A life dedicated to having a relationship with Jesus is like playing in the fairway. It saves you from pain and struggle so that you have more energy for the things that really count in life. Just think of all the energy that is wasted by lying and the path of chaos that it creates. You waste energy trying to remember whom you lied to and what the lies were. It is just so much more peaceful and empowering to live in truth. When you have accepted Jesus by faith, you can begin to change your life in positive, constructive ways. You become a new person. And it shows in all kinds of ways.

Years ago, my brother went out for an afternoon of golf. Because he was alone, the golf pro put him in a foursome with three golfers he had never met before. It was a warm afternoon and, as the round progressed, the other golfers proceeded to drink more and more beer to quench their thirst. With each beer, their language and demeanor became livelier. Through it all, my brother was a great example of Christ. He was friendly and full of grace. Yet he didn't engage in their less-than-desirable behavior. In addition, he was playing lousy. He was shanking shots left and right. After about twelve holes of this kind of play, one of the golfers came up to my brother and asked, "Are you a Christian?" "Yes," my brother replied. "Why do you ask?" "Because anyone who could play as bad as you without swearing must be a Christian!"

It is a funny story, but it also illustrates a powerful truth: Being a follower of Christ means that you can live life differently. Spiritually, you can live in the fairway, keeping out of unnecessary troubles and heartache. The Bible says it this way:

Instead, there must be a spiritual renewal of your thoughts and attitudes. You must display a new nature because you are a new person, created in God's likeness— righteous, holy, and true.

(Ephesians 4:23–24)

Over the years, many people have described this life transformation as being "born again." While this phrase has taken a beating over the years, it was a term originated by Jesus.

In the book of John, chapter 3, Jesus encountered a very religious person. His name was Nicodemus. Today, he would just be called Nick. Nick was one of the highest trained religious leaders in Israel at that time. He belonged to a group of religious leaders that was deeply opposed to the teachings of Christ. After hearing the truth of Jesus, Nick wanted to question Him. He secretly met Jesus one evening to discuss his life philosophy. Nick knew that Jesus was a very special teacher with deep insight.

It was at this time that Jesus made the statement that would characterize the life transformation that happens when people accept God's forgiveness. He said, "I assure you this, unless you are born again, you can never see the Kingdom of God" (v.3). Nick, despite his extensive understanding of Old Testament Scripture, was perplexed and believed that Jesus was suggesting that he would need literally to be reincarnated in his mothers womb. *"Humans can reproduce only human life, but the Holy Spirit gives new life from heaven,"* Jesus assured him (John 3:6).

It is a rebirth that happens in your heart and spirit. You are the same person physically, but you are different on the inside. When you accept this rebirth, it is important to begin transforming your life into the image of Jesus' life. Begin to play life in the fairway!

What does this kind of life look like? Many people believe that the Bible is full of rules, but that is an oversimplification. The truth is that only a small percentage of the Bible is rules for living. These are the *do*s and *don't*s, such as the Ten Commandments. They are a small but very important part of the Bible. They are much like the rule of gravity: You can try to break it, but it will probably break you first. They are crucial to living in the fairway.

Fairway Commandments
Exodus 20:1–17

Don't Worship Anyone but God
God does not want our focus to be on anyone but Him, not only because He deserves it, but also because putting our worship and trust in other people will only lead to disappointment and heartbreak.

Don't Make Idols of Any Kind

God doesn't want us to focus on "stuff" that is temporary and passing. Money and the commodities it can buy are fleeting and not eternal. Trust in the God who has passed the test of time.

Don't Misuse the Name of God

God is deserving of honor and respect. Taking His name lightly and using it in vain shows deep disrespect and indicates that we do not really cherish His greatness, power, and love.

Remember to Keep God's Day Special

Essentially, God has said, "Keep one day of the week to focus on Me." Life is too complicated and fast-paced. God says slow down and smell the roses. This will extend your life and make it sweeter!

Honor Your Mom and Dad

Our relationship with God is a vertical relationship, but He also encourages us to be careful to respect the relationships we have here on earth—horizontal relationships. Relationships with our parents are some of the trickiest relationships we have. Be sure to honor them.

Don't Murder

Controlling your anger is difficult and worthy of special attention. God values life and reminds us that we do not have the power to take someone else's life unjustly.

Don't Engage in Sex Outside of Marriage

While this may not be en vogue in our culture, God says that sex outside of marriage can cause emotional and physical damage to you and others. God designed sex to be enjoyed inside the arena of marriage. Only then is sex at its best.

Don't Steal

A godly society is built upon trust. When you take what doesn't belong to you, it breaks trust and causes cynicism and anger. It also harms innocent people and shows great selfishness.

Don't Say Something That Isn't True

The Bible says that every word we say will be remembered. Speak the truth and you save yourself and others a lot of pain.

Don't Be Greedy for What Belongs to Others

It can be difficult to see all the material goods that are around you and not covet what others have that you don't. God reminds us that contentment is an important part of enjoying life and maximizing the moment.

Live Life in the Fairway!

The majority of the Bible is "principles for living," not commandments. These principles are ideals and ideas that are applicable in every circumstance of life. They are perhaps represented best by what the Bible calls the "fruits of the spirit." In a physical sense, fruit is the visible proof of a tree. When you see an apple hanging from a branch, you know that the tree is an apple tree. An apple tree can't produce peaches. If it did, it would be a peach tree. So it is with you and me. The Bible encourages us to observe the fruit of our lives. Are we individuals who show visible proof of being followers of Christ? These fruits are principles for healthy living. They are benefits that we can have in our lives as Christians.

Fairway Living #1: Love
God is love. We are called to love also. The Bible says that love is how people will know that we are followers of Christ. We are to be examples of love!

Fairway Living #2: Joy

Joy is the happiness that comes from seeing the world through a new, more positive perspective.

Fairway Living #3: Peace

This is the inner freedom you feel when you are forgiven and living life in the fairway.

Fairway Living #4: Kindness

This world is short on kindness. Kindness is the manner in which we treat people. Instead of being cynical and short, we can be welcoming and gracious.

Fairway Living #5: Goodness

We can do the right thing. Some of us have a harder time with this than others. The fact of the matter is that when we are "born again" we have the ability, through Jesus, to do what is right.

Fairway Living #6: Faithfulness

The world is full of flaky people. You can't count on them to keep their word. But living in Christ means being a person who can be counted on.

Fairway Living #7: Gentleness

In this rough and tumble world, people can get bullied, but Christians are called to be gentle with others. Gentleness was a hallmark of Jesus. He was a gentle and approachable person. The Bible tells us that children loved Him and felt His gentle spirit.

Fairway Living #8: Self-control

Controlling what we say and do can be difficult. The Bible says that controlling what we say is the hardest job of all! But we have control over our lives because all things are possible through the power of God. (See Philippians 4:13.)

Sand Traps and Water Hazards

Sand Traps and Water Hazards

Golf courses are designed to punish certain kinds of golfers. Most people think that the person who hits the ball the farthest wins. But golf course designers know that some people can hit the ball long, so they will build a hazard into the golf course to make it difficult for long hitters. It is not uncommon to have a fairway bunker at 250 yards, as a threat to long hitters. Challenges are designed into each green, making it downright scary to attempt a long shot at the pin. Women golfers are particularly good at understanding this; they have no problem hitting a more controlled, shorter shot.

But men have a problem with this. We consider every hazard a direct challenge. I can think of numerous times when I have stood looking at a tiny green surrounded by water, sand, and tall rough, and have thought to myself, "You can't scare me. I am going for it!" Usually this ends in disaster. But at least I never backed down. (It's a guy thing.) To be honest, most golfers will tell you that the hazards and traps are what makes a golf course interesting. If you had wide-open spaces and could hit the ball anywhere you wanted without fear of punishment, then it would take the challenge out of the course. That is why the most revered courses in the world, like Augusta or Pebble Beach, are so difficult. People like to know that they can beat the best courses in the world. The reason people dislike hazards is that they must take a penalty stroke to get out of it. At the very least, it can be tricky and treacherous to get out of the sand. Many players have gained plenty of strokes trying to hit a ball out of the sand.

Life has its challenges, too. Sometimes it even seems like it is designed to punish us and bring us down. The hazards that life throws at us generally originate from two different sources. The first source of pain and suffering is the devil. While some people question the existence of the devil, I assure you that he is quite real. The Bible says that he is like a lion, wanting to kill and destroy you and me. The devil has limited power. He is not as powerful as God—not even close. He is a created creature, and he does not have the power to overwhelm God or Christ's followers—at least, not without our permission. The second source of hazards in life is our own actions and decisions. These are by far the more common sources of pain and suffering. I think that people give the devil more credit than he deserves. Most of the time, we bring problems on ourselves.

When we fall into a life bunker, it is always discouraging and embarrassing. But we don't have to live there. We can find our way out of the bunker and onto the green. The answer is in a simple word with powerful implications. In some ways, it is the most important word in the Bible. The word is *grace. Grace* is the word the Bible uses to describe God's ongoing forgiveness toward us. When you grasp the concept of grace, you will really understand the power of living a Christian life. Grace can be best understood by examining what it is not. We cannot earn forgiveness by being good people. That only helps us in the present; it doesn't deal with the past. Besides, if we could earn forgiveness, then we could brag that we were great. Grace is not about earning forgiveness; it is about accepting forgiveness even though we do not deserve it.

> *And so God can always point to us as examples of the incredible wealth of his favor and kindness toward us, as shown in all he has done for us through Christ Jesus. God saved you by his special favor when you believed. And you can't take credit for this; it is a gift from God. Salvation is not a reward for the good things we have done, so none of us can boast about it.* (Ephesians 2:7–9)

People often have a hard time understanding how it is to God's advantage to give forgiveness as a free gift. We want to earn it, to feel like we are independent and self-sufficient. But a relationship with God is not about independence or dependence. It is an interdependent relationship. God desires a relationship with you. And you need a relationship with him. It will make your life more fulfilling and free you from the shadows of the past.

There is a path before each person that seems right, but it ends in death.
> (Proverbs 14:12)

A few years ago, I was golfing with a friend who did not consider himself a religious person, and we discussed a relationship with Jesus. He casually mentioned that he had a difficult time believing that he could be forgiven. He had a vivid memory of the things he had done in his past, and he knew that his behavior didn't match the goodness of God. It was at that time that I explained the grace of Jesus: I told him that we are forgiven when we accept Jesus. We do not have to earn His love; it is ever present. This was a tremendous awakening for my friend. He had grown up believing that only religious people are able to know God and go to heaven. The truth is that forgiveness is for sinners. The Bible reminds us that we are all sinners, and we all need to be forgiven.

For all have sinned; all fall short of God's glorious standard. Yet now God in his gracious kindness declares us not guilty. He has done this through Christ Jesus, who has freed us by taking away our sins. For God sent Jesus to take the punishment for our sins and to satisfy God's anger against us. We are made right with God when we believe that Jesus shed his blood, sacrificing his life for us. (Romans 3:23–25)

Does this mean that you can accept forgiveness and then continue to keep your negative habits and live for yourself? Why would you want to? That would be like never wanting to play golf correctly, being content to go from rough to bunker to water hazard. It takes all the fun out of life. If you accept the forgiveness of Christ, you are free to start a new life.

Well then, if we emphasize faith, does this mean that we can forget about the law? Of course not! In fact, only when we have faith do we truly fulfill the law.
(Romans 3:31)

Once we are forgiven, we then want to do the right thing because we are grateful for the new start. And because living the goodness of God is a happier, more peaceful way to live, we can play the fairway and stay out of the rough!

Mulligans, Handicaps, and Gimmes

4

Mulligans, Handicaps, and Gimmes

*T*here is no concept more beloved among weekend duffers than the concept of the mulligan. For those of you who are unfamiliar with the concept, let me explain. A *mulligan* is a free stroke given to a golfer when he or she has previously knocked a shot into the woods, water, sand, or some other hazard. It is common for some casual golfers to use one or two "mulligans" in a round of 18 holes. A mulligan is a freebie. Golfers around the world are forever grateful to Mr. Mulligan, wherever he may be, for coming up with the concept. While I have no idea why the word *mulligan* came to be associated with a free stroke, I think it probably happened like this: There was likely a man named Mulligan who was eternally shanking his drive into the woods. He would then call for a freebie and take another shot. After some time his friends probably began to either get tired of giving him the advantage, or they were just as bad as he was, and started taking "mulligans" for themselves. The concept of getting a "do-over" is nothing new. God created the first "mulligan" when He designed a plan for imperfect people to experience forgiveness.

The most memorable mulligan I ever took was about ten years ago. I was playing a golf course in Oregon, accompanied by my wife. The course had a winding river through the middle of it and the holes criss-crossed the river at different points. It was a beautiful course, with ducks and geese wandering about. On the sixth hole, the river ran across the fairway about 195 yards from the tee. On the other side of the river lay the green. I had it in my mind that I could land my ball on the green if I hit a good stroke. So I wound up and took a good swing. I knew that if I were going to clear the river I would have to hit the ball 215 yards. It took off like a shot. It was flying low and straight—I had a great shot.

As it began to descend, I noticed that it was heading for a group of ducks sitting by the river. My concern was that it would clear the river; I should have been concerned that it would clear the ducks. As the ball came down at a rapid pace, it entered one of the ducks that didn't move quickly enough, killing him. When your ball is accidentally embedded in a duck, that is technically called an "unplayable lie." I was forced to take a mulligan.

Our shortcomings and mistakes are not always as humorous and temporary as those in golf. (Although the duck didn't think it was humorous or temporary.) Sometimes when we make mistakes, people get hurt and lives are damaged. Think of all the lives that have been hurt, words that were spoken in anger, and actions that were taken and cannot be undone. Once we make a mistake in life, it is impossible to change it. We can make every effort to correct our mistakes and take appropriate measures to see that the damage is limited, but the fact remains, we have blown it. Many people say time heals all wounds, but that doesn't always hold true. While some people can forget their mistakes and perhaps even pretend they don't exist, the mistakes take their toll. Even if people forget—and they seldom do—God has a much better memory.

As we discussed in the last chapter, God in His very nature is good. He is always doing what is right and correct. This makes Him the ultimate example of righteousness as well as an impartial judge. The idea that God is looking over your shoulder, keeping score, is enough to make many people cringe. It only reinforces their image of God as a heavenly killjoy. But the Bible describes God differently. The Bible paints an image of a God who loves and is full of forgiveness. His standard is perfection, because that is His nature. But He also understands that we are not capable of perfection, especially retroactive perfection that allows us to change past behavior. We are limited to the moment in which we are currently living.

Accepting Jesus Is Like Taking a Mulligan.
You Get Another Chance!

In golf, there is a system for making the competition even, called a "handicap." Less experienced golfers are given a few strokes of grace to help them compare their scores with better players. Jesus dying on the cross is like a golf handicap. It makes up the difference between God's goodness and our sinfulness!

In our relationship with God, it is not our inexperience that separates us, but our own imperfections and sin. As long as we are separated from God by our sin, there is no human way to make up the difference. But remember, God is love. He doesn't want people to miss heaven and a relationship with Him here on earth. So He created a path to forgiveness that will help people who have sinned and missed the mark—that's all of us. He sent His Son Jesus to pay the ultimate price for us.

> *God showed how much he loved us by sending his only Son into the world so that we might have eternal life through him. This is real love.* (1 John 4:9–10)

Through Jesus dying on the cross, we are able to have a relationship with God. Because of His loving nature, God has allowed us to be forgiven for the mistakes we have made by simply associating ourselves with His Son. If we recognize that we can't do it by ourselves and if we accept Jesus as our Mediator, we can be forgiven. How can a person receive Christ? The Bible shows us the way to forgiveness.

...Admit your need.

No one is able to earn his or her forgiveness. Even people like Billy Graham and the late Mother Teresa have admitted that they need God's forgiveness. It is okay for you and me to need forgiveness too. But you have to realize that you need His forgiveness; He won't force you. It is a decision.

...Turn your life around.

The Bible uses the word *repent*, which means to turn away from your negative habits, attitudes, and actions, and follow the teachings of Jesus. Through prayer and Bible study you can begin to see the areas of your life that are holding you back. Positive life change is possible.

...Believe that Jesus died for you.

He paid the ultimate price for you. He took the first step, making it possible for us to experience forgiveness and spiritual freedom. Nothing happens without faith. Our relationships in business, friendship, and family are all based upon faith and trust. Once you realize you have already been living by faith, you can begin to put your faith in someone who never changes. God is ultimately reliable and faithful. The Bible says this:

> *But God showed his great love for us by sending Christ to die for us while we were still sinners.*   (Romans 5:8)

...Invite Jesus Christ in.

While the Bible is clear that God wants to have a relationship with you, He will not force you to serve Him. He is not looking for robots. We were created with a free will and we must choose to be part of God's family. While it is an important decision, it is not a difficult process. You need only to invite Jesus into your life. The Bible says this:

> *If you confess with your mouth that Jesus is Lord and believe in your heart that God raised him from the dead, you will be saved. For it is by believing in your heart that you are made right with God, and it is by confessing with your mouth that you are saved...."Anyone who believes in Him will not be disappointed."* (Romans 10:9–11)

Forgiveness Is a Gimme!
You Can Accept It as a Free Gift!

The question, then, is "What is the cost for accepting this gift of forgiveness?" Americans are always leery of anything that is free. It is almost as though we have been conditioned to question anything that is a giveaway. Golfers understand the concept of free. In golf, it is called a "gimme." If a casual golfer has his ball sitting within a few inches of the cup, his playing partners have the right to allow him to pick up the ball without putting out. This ensures that the player will not get any additional strokes and embarrassment by missing an easy putt.

The gift of salvation is a gimme. The Bible says that salvation is a free gift. Now, for our own good, God asks us to leave our old mistakes, habits, and attitudes behind and follow a path that will develop us into people who are more like Jesus. While it seems strange to imagine that we would not want to give up the negative habits that hold us back, we humans *are* strange. We often hold tight to habits that slowly destroy us, like smoking and eating too much fatty food. On an emotional level, it is no different. We want to continue to hold tight to what we feel comfortable doing, even if that action, attitude, or emotion is slowly breaking us down. Giving up negative behavior and following a path toward the attitudes, actions, and emotions of Christ is required because it's good for us. Losing negative habits, no matter how comfortable, is like having a huge weight lifted off your shoulders. And it costs you nothing. Forgiveness is a gimme!

Jesus Has the Power to Forgive Because He Conquered Death!

Once you and I have accepted this forgiveness, we are able to experience a spiritual "mulligan." We are able to leave the disappointment and bitterness of past hurts and mistakes behind and move on. We can be free from the negative habits and sins that have held us prisoner. The Bible says that sin makes us slaves to negative habits; forgiveness sets us free. It is a fact that Jesus rose from the dead. This is important because Jesus paid the price for our sins. His apostles gave their lives because they believed in the fact that Jesus rose from the dead. If it were not true, they could have easily disbanded and each gone their own way. But they knew it was true because they saw Him with their own eyes. He lived a perfect life, died for our sins, and then conquered death. He played by the rules of this earth and still won! Now, He has the moral and legal authority to set people free. It is within your power to accept His forgiveness. You need to make a decision.

You can make a decision right now to accept the forgiveness of Jesus. God does not require that you be in a church or be speaking with a pastor or priest. You need only admit that you have made mistakes, that you have sinned, and that you want to accept the forgiveness that is available through the life of Jesus. If you are not ready, that is okay. Keep reading to discover more about what being a follower of Jesus really means. It is important that you make an informed decision. But if you are at the point in your life where you are ready to be free from your past mistakes, then you can accept the forgiveness of Jesus right now. Because many people feel uneasy praying to God at first, I have taken the liberty of giving you an example of what a prayer for salvation might sound like. If you like, you can pray this prayer aloud for yourself. It has meaning, and you can be sure that God hears you.

> *God, I recognize that I have made mistakes in the past and that I will make mistakes in the future. I see now that I need to be forgiven for my sins to have a close relationship with You. I want to know You and to follow You. I want to be on Your team. I am ready to be free. I won't live in the past, but will focus on how You and I can create a better future instead. Please forgive my sins. I accept Jesus into my heart and accept Your forgiveness. I am a new person. Amen.*

If you prayed that prayer, you are forgiven. Your mistakes are now in the past; Jesus has already been punished on your behalf. He has made you a new person.

5

Making Solid Contact

Making Solid Contact

*T*here is no better feeling in golf than making a solid connection with the ball. Good golfers will tell you that when you do it right, it seems almost effortless. Watching the ball jump off your club and scream down the fairway is a terrific sensation. Golf legend suggests that everyone has at least one shot in a round that keeps him or her coming back for more. And in my experience, that is true. Even when I have played poorly, there were always a few shots that encouraged me. These are the strokes I choose to remember. Great golfers are those who make great connection with the golf ball on a regular basis. They learn how to make solid contact and then condition themselves to repeat the process. I have not yet learned how to do that consistently, but I keep trying.

My instructor tells me that part of the challenge is making time to practice on the range. Through repetition, you can begin to feel the correct swing. Then, when you hit the ball in a game situation, you will know when you are hitting the ball correctly. You will be in a positive groove. And it's true: After I've spent time practicing, I have a much better feeling for where the ball is going. (I have found that most golfers don't really know where the ball is going, but they are afraid to admit that.) Time spent hitting ball after ball has done wonders for golfers like Tiger Woods, David Duvall, and Vijay Singh. They practice more than other golfers, and it shows in the consistent contact they make with the ball.

Just as making solid contact with the golf ball is important, so is making contact with God. As in any relationship, making contact with God is all about communication. It is keeping in touch. Some people struggle to understand how we can communicate with God when we can't see Him. However, in this day and age it is becoming easier to understand how God intends for us to communicate with Him. With the addition of cellular phones, we are able to be in contact with our friends and family from almost anywhere. Cellular technology is designed and managed by mere humans, yet we can receive a signal through the air and it will find us if we are on the eighteenth hole of Pebble Beach or putting on a course in Scotland. The technology is amazing. Right now, as I am writing, I have a cellular phone that can be activated by the sound of my voice. If I say, "Call home," the phone identifies the phrase that I have programmed into it and calls my home. No hands are necessary. Now, if we can figure this technology out, imagine how much more advanced God is! God was voice-activated long before it was cool. The Bible says that we are able to connect with God. This makes having a relationship with Him possible.

The most personal way for us to connect with God is through prayer. One of the defining characteristics of love is that it wants to communicate. Because God loves you, He wants to talk. Prayer allows you and me to talk to God, and it allows God to talk to us. Although some religious traditions have made prayer no more than a religious exercise, prayer is intended to be something less formal and more personal.

Just as making contact is important in golf, so it is in your relationship with Jesus. There is something very special that happens in conversations with God. I have found that I become more aware of my own feelings. When I vocalize the issues, victories, and struggles that I am facing, I am more able to see how God is working in my life. I am also allowing God to begin working on some of the issues that seem too big for me. Prayer releases the power of God. Studies are beginning to show that people who pray are healthier, happier people. They are able to deal with problems better and to give seemingly insurmountable problems to God. Prayer helps you let go of negative energy and create positive momentum. *There is power in prayer.*

Many people struggle to understand prayer because they don't feel anything when they pray. But those feelings are just a matter of making consistent connection. Remember that God exists. The Bible says that those who look for Him can find God easily. You will not be left alone if you are praying to God. If you are a person who has not prayed in many years, or have never regularly practiced the power of prayer, Jesus provided an example of how to pray. He did not give us this prayer to be mindlessly repeated, although these words are as good as any; He gave us these words to give us a structure for our own prayers. Here is the outline He gave us in the book of Matthew. If you observe this outline, it will help you to begin experiencing powerful prayer.

> *Pray like this: Our Father in heaven, may your name be honored. May your Kingdom come soon. May your will be done here on earth, just as it is in heaven. Give us our food for today, and forgive us our sins, just as we have forgiven those who have sinned against us. And don't let us yield to temptation, but deliver us from the evil one.* (Matthew 6:9–13)

Communication Principles

...Speak directly to God.

Jesus said to address God personally. This makes sense when you remember that God loves us and wants to communicate with us.

...Praise God.

Jesus honored God. This is important for God and for us. It helps us to remember that we have been loved and forgiven by God. We have much to be thankful to God for. He is awesome; we should vocalize our thoughts about how great He is.

...Give God daily control of your life.

Jesus wanted us to invite God to bring His kingdom here on earth. In other words, "God, You are in charge of my life today. What can I do to serve You today?" I like to start each day with one question and to ask this question repeatedly throughout the day: "Jesus, what can I do for You today?" This helps me to be alert and aware of how I can improve my attitudes, words, and actions.

Don't copy the behavior and customs of this world, but let God transform you into a new person by changing the way you think. Then you will know what God wants you to do, and you will know how good and pleasing and perfect his will really is. (Romans 12:2)

...Ask God for what you need.

Jesus encouraged us to ask God on a daily basis for the things we need in our lives. God is very interested in our daily lives. It is okay to ask for the physical things that we need. He is not offended by these requests. But take careful notice that prayer is not only about asking for what we need. There are many other things that are just as important.

...Ask for forgiveness.

Jesus knew that we were going to be making mistakes, and He encouraged us to daily ask for forgiveness. Daily asking for forgiveness allows us to make a new start. We can all use a life "mulligan." Every day is a new day—that is why the Bible says that we are "new creations" when we are forgiven by God.

...We need to forgive others.

Jesus encouraged us to let go of the anger and disappointment that others have caused. It is not healthy for us to carry all that bitterness and resentment. Through daily forgiving others, we can let go of the past disappointments and move toward a better future. We can't control other people anyway!

...Pray about the issues that you struggle with.

Jesus understands that we are tempted. Temptation by itself is not unusual—but when we succumb to temptation, we become slaves to negative habits. We all have habits, attitudes, and negative patterns that hold us back. Some are more obvious—such as alcohol, drugs, and illicit sex—but words and negative mental patterns can be just as destructive as physical sins. God wants us to deal with baggage.

...Pray in the name of Jesus.

Jesus is our Mediator. He was the one who paid the price for your mistakes. By praying in Jesus' name, you are reminding yourself, God, and the devil that you are with Jesus. You are on His team. When you pray, "In Jesus' name," you have not just made a vain repetition; you have made a strong statement of faith!

For there is only one God and one Mediator who can reconcile God and people. He is the man Christ Jesus.

(1 Timothy 2:5)

…Listen.

Prayer also involves taking time to listen to what God might want to say to you. God can give you great ideas, new attitudes, and a deeper connection with the emotions you are feeling through a time of quiet reflection.

That simply means asking God, "God, I need a new idea," and sitting quietly to see what you and God can dream up. If you are struggling with your marriage, you need to pray, "God, help me better understand what my spouse needs." Then quietly reflect about how you can help meet your spouse's needs. You will find that your best moments of prayer are in quiet reflection.

Read the Bible.
It Is Your Life Manual!

There are many questions in life that can be answered without prayer. When in doubt, read the instructions! The Bible is the handbook for godly living. It contains wisdom for raising kids, creating a happy marriage, and ensuring business success. It even has wisdom for making money! It can't tell you how to correct your slice, but it can help you deal with your anger when you do slice! The wisdom of the Bible is so big and vast that it can be intimidating. Here is the best way to get started.

...Get a Bible in an accurate modern translation.

There is nothing about the King James version of the Bible that makes it more holy. The Bible was originally written in Greek and Hebrew. Everything we read is a translation into English. You will get more out of the Bible if you read a translation that is both accurate and understandable. I currently read the *New Living Translation*, but there are many excellent translations.

...Start reading the book of John.

The book of John is in the New Testament and tells the story of Jesus Christ. Read the words of Christ. They will transform your life.

...Read something every day.

If the Bible is a handbook for life—and it is—then it can help you solve the tough problems you face each day. Why not start the day right by reading a few verses of Proverbs? Reading a Psalm daily can be a great idea, too!

...Find a good Bible study.

Eventually, you will need to grow stronger and be more informed in your faith. Find a Bible study group and get to know the depth of wisdom in the Bible.

6

Playing in a Foursome

Playing in a Foursome

Golf is not nearly as fun when you play by yourself. Even though golf is a game played between the course and each player, it is more enjoyable to walk the course with a group of friends. Some of the best days of my life have been spent on the golf course with the blue sky above, surrounded by friends having a great time laughing with and at each other. I smile just thinking about it. One moment is particularly memorable. I had gathered with some old friends to play a round of golf. We were having a good time telling stories and generally teasing each other. My friend was warming up, taking a few practice swings in mid-air, while waiting for the group in front of us to finish. As he was warming up, he was looking at the rest of us, telling us a story. But as he came through his swing, he made a miscalculation and hit dirt. Hitting dirt is an understatement—he took a slice out of the turf that was at least three inches wide and six inches long. It was hilarious. But it got funnier. As the turf left the earth, it headed straight for the head of my brother, who was standing right next to me. The mud on the bottom worked like glue as the turf stuck to his face. We lost it, and we all rolled on the ground in laughter. It was a great moment, the kind you can't experience by yourself. Being with great friends makes a big difference.

The concept of playing in a foursome is not exclusive to golf. The Bible talks about the power of teamwork. The biblical term is *fellowship,* but the concept is similar. Life is more fun when you don't make the journey alone. Accountability groups are nothing new; people in churches, businesses, and support groups have used them for centuries. In essence, it is really recreating the idea of family. The Bible understands that we do not always have the most supportive and encouraging family situations. That is why Jesus encouraged His disciples to consider other Christ followers as family. We are brothers and sisters in Jesus' family.

I have traveled to different countries all over the world, but I have always found that I have a family of believers who accept and welcome me as their brother. Jesus had twelve disciples with whom He spent His most valuable time. He poured His life into those men. He laughed, cried, and lived with them. They experienced life together. We need that kind of support, too! You and I need to find a group of people with whom we can grow in our Christian walk. I'll call it a Fellowship Foursome. But there is no magic number needed to get the maximum benefit from fellowship. Studies prove that most adults don't even have one or two really good friends; just beginning to reach out to others is a positive step.

Benefits of Fellowship Groups

...They help you grow.
It is important to have people in your life who are close enough to you to tell you the truth. Good Christian friends can let you know when you are off base in your attitudes

and actions. This is really important for those of us who don't have this thing called life perfected yet. Surround yourself with people who want to grow. Not everyone is progressing in the same direction as you. Find some who are and develop those relationships.

...They keep you from making obvious mistakes.

Accountability is a very important part of spiritual growth. We all struggle with private issues that hold us back. Since the Christian life is characterized by godly virtues, it takes time to change; and we need other people to support us in the transformation process without making us feel like we are failing. It is important that you become accountable to someone. I like to encourage people to use this book as the beginning of an accountability foursome. The person who gave you this book cared enough about you to encourage you toward a relationship with God. That person can be a great place to start. Ask him or her to help hold you accountable in your walk with God. Then, as you share this book with others, you can help them be accountable. Believe me: Accountability works! You are not meant to be an island unto yourself.

...They encourage you.

We need to build each other up. Looking at the world around us, it is obvious that we need more people who are building one another up. The habit of the world is to tear people down to make ourselves feel better. Don't do it! Be dedicated to building others up! Christians are called to support each other. Fellowship is not just for you to feel better; it is also so that you can support and encourage each other. The most popular person in any room is the person who is listening, encouraging, and interested in other people. Christ was the ultimate in unselfishness. He is our model.

...They make life more fun.

Not all of life is meant to be serious. Remember that one of the biblical virtues is joy! I will admit that church people are not always known for being joyful people, but that is only because they are not always living in the freedom that God wants for them. They are stuck in old habits. New life calls for joy. You need to surround yourself with people you enjoy. True joy doesn't come from sharing a beer with a bunch of old friends. It comes from connecting with people.

If you are hiding yourself behind alcohol and empty pursuits, you are going to have a hard time getting to know other people. And they are going to have a hard time getting to know you. Step out from behind the mask that we are all tempted to wear: the mask of perfection. You don't have it all together, and neither does anyone else. Just be yourself and have a good time.

Sharing Your Faith

Christ encouraged His followers to reach out to others and include them. Once you understand the importance of a relationship with God, you have responsibility to tell others what God has done for you. You don't need to be obnoxious and overbearing. But as with anything that is worthwhile, you will want to share it with others. How can you best share your faith?

...Simply tell people you are a Christian.
By making a statement of faith, you have made a stand for what you believe in. In addition, you are creating a system of accountability for yourself.

...Invite a friend to church or Bible study.

This is a great way to introduce people to faith in God in a non-threatening way.

...Introduce your friends to the wisdom of the Bible.

The actual words of Christ are powerful and life-transforming. Start in the book of John in the New Testament. You will be amazed at the power of Jesus.

...Give this book to your friends.

By giving this book, or other books like it, you can introduce them to faith in a way that will give them an overview of the purpose and life of Jesus. You can even keep three in your golf bag to give to friends you meet on the course. It is an easy way to break the ice.

...Be a living example.

If you are living the principles of Jesus Christ, you will be an obvious example to the people around you. You may not have to say anything: They will notice all by themselves! Remember that your actions speak louder than words.

7

The
Clubhouse

The Clubhouse

*E*very great golf course has a first-class clubhouse. If it doesn't have a great club-house, it probably isn't a great golf course yet. Any golfer can tell you that the clubhouse is an important part of the golfing experience. It is the place where everyone gathers after a day of golf to swap stories about the battle against the course. It is a gathering place where friends come together. A great clubhouse has great food and a welcoming, relaxed attitude. It does not matter how old or new the clubhouse is: It is all about the way it welcomes its golfers.

Every Christ follower needs to be part of a "spiritual clubhouse." Actually, the word *clubhouse* is not a completely accurate word to describe the kind of community believers need. The word *clubhouse* sounds exclusive and membership oriented. The kind of community that the Bible talks about is *inclusive* and open to all who want to be a part.

The idea of church is not just a modern concept. Synagogues and churches of all kinds have existed since before the time of Christ. But Christ changed the concept of churches from places of exclusivity into places of spiritual growth and inclusion. People have long fought the idea of "organized religion" and often for good reason. Organized religion is not what we are talking about here. We are talking about a return to the concept of church as it was described in the New Testament: a place where people could go to find spiritual wisdom, comfort, support, and friendship; a place where imperfect people come together to learn more about the words and life of Christ; a place where people join together as a community to reach out to those who are hurting, hungry, tired, and broken. Jesus intended for churches to be places that would be an extension of His love and grace. While you may not have realized it, communities like this exist all over the world. There are churches in your area that seek to model standards of biblical living. To better help you understand what a Christian community should look like, I have included the biblical description of the church of Jesus.

> *They joined with other believers and devoted themselves to the apostles' teaching and fellowship, sharing in the Lord's Supper and in prayer. A deep sense of awe came over them all, and the apostles performed many miraculous signs and wonders. And all the believers met together constantly and shared everything they had. They sold their possessions and shared the proceeds with those in need. They worshiped together at the Temple each day, met in homes for the Lord's Supper, and shared their meals with great joy and generosity—all the while praising God and enjoying the goodwill of all the people. And each day the Lord added to their group those who were being saved.* (Acts 2:42–47)

Healthy Churches....

...Share the grace of Jesus Christ.

The Bible says that salvation is a free gift. You cannot earn it. The church you choose should affirm and teach the grace of Jesus. Even churches can lose sight of the fact that we are all sinners saved only by grace. Find a church that is inclusive and loving, and become an active part of it.

...Encourage spiritual growth.

The Bible says that Christ's followers should exemplify fruitful virtues that show people they have a relationship with Jesus. Christians need to be part of a community that will help them to develop in their spiritual life. Some people accept the forgiveness of Jesus and then never experience the benefits of Christian living. Accepting forgiveness will help you get into heaven, but from now until then, what will your life look like? Following the truths of Jesus will help you enjoy life on earth to the maximum. Find a church that teaches biblical truth.

...Have healthy fellowship.

The Bible reminds us that we need each other. For reasons described in the previous chapter, fellowship is very important. Find a church that has people in your age and interest group, and connect with those people: Make friends: You will be glad you did.

…Encourage believers to participate.

Somewhere along the line, attending church became a spectator sport. It was not intended to be this way. We are all gifted with special talents and gifts that can help the church reach out to people. Just as the body is made up of different parts, so the church is designed with different people who serve different purposes.

Get involved in a church. Teach a class, organize a fund-raiser, reach out to your friends, or volunteer to mow your neighbor's lawn. Find something you enjoy doing and do it! (For further reading on this issue, read my book, *Change Your World.*)

…Encourage people to use their resources.

Many people shy away from churches that ask them to contribute on a financial and resource level. But the Bible is clear that contributing your resources is necessary to being part of a community. Don't be overly sensitive to contributing in this way. There are many ways to contribute, even if you are not a person with a lot of money. The Bible says that God values the position of your heart and attitude, not your pocketbook.

God doesn't need your money; He wants only to know that money and resources are not as important to you as He is. By regularly contributing, you can continually remind yourself that God comes first. There are many great books and Scriptures that will help you find out what the Bible says about the concept of tithing and contributing resources.

19th Hole

As this book comes to an end, let me encourage you to read and study more about the life of Christ. This book is just a beginning. There are many concepts here that need to be read over in order to fully understand and appreciate them. Don't be afraid to use this as a handbook and continually reference it in the future. You should know that I will be praying for you and others who read this book. My prayer is that you will know Jesus in a personal way and that you will have a happy, fulfilled life. Maybe someday we will see each other on the golf course.

Oh, by the way, if golf is a joyful part of your life, I believe you may be able to golf in heaven. And if you ask Him, maybe God will play with you. See you there.

> *There is salvation in no one else! There is no other name in all of heaven for people to call on to save them.*   (Acts 4:12)

How to Use This Book

How to Use This Book

G reat golf is a metaphor for great living. While these biblical principles are simple, they also have great depth. You may need to reread it for greater understanding. Use this as a handbook that you can reference over and over again.

If you are already a follower of Christ, share this book with at least three others who you know need to hear the basic message of Jesus. Better yet, keep three in your golf bag, so that you will never be without a resource to share with those you see on the golf course.

Our desire is to share the life-transforming words and life of Jesus Christ. My prayer is that this book will be used for that purpose.

About the Author

*D*avid Curry is a lifelong "duffer." The layman's definition of *duffer* is, "Someone who has played golf for a long time, but never seems to improve." Recently, David has renewed his commitment to improve his game and has begun taking lessons. His golf instructor asked that his name not be published in this book for professional reasons. David wants to affirm that his instructor is in no way responsible for David's golf game.

David is also the president of the Foundation for Grace, an organization dedicated to helping pastors and churches reach the unreached of their communities. He has an international ministry helping pastors and leaders reach their full potential. David speaks to thousands of pastors in Peru and South America each year through his Pastoral Leadership Conferences.

David is known for his practical and uplifting speaking style. His honest and direct approach has helped thousands deal with the most difficult issues in leadership and Christian living.

He is the author of the book, *Change Your World*.

David and his wife, Kathleen, live in Tacoma, Washington, with their two sons, Jack and Cole.

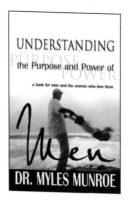